EAT SMART

FRUITS

Louise Spilsbury

www.heinemann.co.uk/library
Visit our website to find out more information about Heinemann Library books.

To order:

 Phone 44 (0) 1865 888066

 Send a fax to 44 (0) 1865 314091

 Visit the Heinemann Bookshop at www.heinemann.co.uk/library to browse our catalogue and order online.

Heinemann Library is an imprint of Capstone Global Library Limited, a company incorporated in England and Wales having its registered office at 7 Pilgrim Street, London, EC4V 6LB – Registered company number: 6695582

"Heinemann" is a registered trademark of Pearson Education Limited, under licence to Capstone Global Library Limited

Edited by Charlotte Guillain and Diyan Leake
Designed by Richard Parker and Manhattan Design
Picture research by Hannah Taylor
Production by Alison Parsons
Originated by Dot Gradations Ltd
Printed and bound in China by CTPS

ISBN 978 0 431066 16 5 (hardback)
13 12 11 10 09
10 9 8 7 6 5 4 3 2 1

British Library Cataloguing in Publication Data
Spilsbury, Louise
   Fruits. - (Eat smart)
   641.3'4

A full catalogue record for this book is available from the British Library.

Acknowledgements
We would like to thank the following for permission to reproduce photographs: © Alamy pp. 7 (Per Karlsson-BKWine.com), 8 (Pedro Luz Cunha), 9 (Inga Spence), 15 (Jupiter Images/Creatas); © FLPA p. 6 (Sunset); © Getty Images p. 19 (Gallo Images/Kenneth Gerhardt); © iStockphoto pp. 1–32 background images; © PA p. 16 (Empics); © Pearson Education Ltd/MM Studios pp. 4, 24, 25 top, 25 bottom, 26, 27 top, 27 bottom, 28, 29 top, 29 bottom; © Photolibrary pp. 5 (Corbis), 12 (Digital Vision), 14 (Stockbyte), 17 (It Stock Royalty Free), 18 (Digital Vision); © Rex Features p. 21 (Sipa Press); © Science Photo Library pp. 10 (Veronique Leplat), 13 (GustoImages); © StockFood UK pp. 11 (Lew Robertson), 20 (FoodPhotography Eising).

Cover photograph reproduced with permission of © Corbis (photocuisine/Y. Bagros).

Every effort has been made to contact copyright holders of material reproduced in this book. Any omissions will be rectified in subsequent printings if notice is given to the publishers.

Disclaimer
All the Internet addresses (URLs) given in this book were valid at the time of going to press. However, due to the dynamic nature of the Internet, some addresses may have changed, or sites may have changed or ceased to exist since publication. While the author and publishers regret any inconvenience this may cause readers, no responsibility for any such changes can be accepted by either the author or the publishers.

CONTENTS

Some words are shown in bold, **like this**. You can find out what they mean by looking in the glossary.

WHAT IS FRUIT?

When people talk about fruit, they usually mean the soft or juicy kinds that you eat as a dessert or snack, such as oranges, apples, or bananas. Scientists say a fruit is the part of a plant that holds its **seeds**.

How many different types of fruit are there?

There are thousands of different types of fruit. They come in different sizes, shapes, and colours, and grow on many different kinds of plants. Plums are a purple fruit with a thin skin and a large single seed, or stone. Oranges have a thick **inedible** skin, or peel, and many seeds inside. You don't eat the seeds of these fruits. But in other fruits, including strawberries and raspberries, the seeds are so small that you eat them, too.

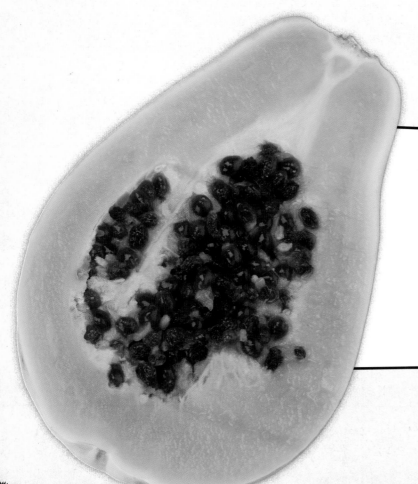

On a plant, a fruit's job is to protect the seeds until they are ripe and fully developed. That is why the seeds of most of the fruits you eat are inside the fruit.

Fruits grow all over the world and are transported to shops and markets so you have a wide range to choose from, including some with interesting names such as dragon fruit or star fruit.

Why is it smart to eat fruits?

It is smart to eat fruits because they contain vitamins and minerals. These are **nutrients** that the human body needs to grow, to develop properly, and to stay healthy. Scientific studies have shown that people who eat a lot of fruit and vegetables may have a lower risk of serious illnesses such as **diabetes** and heart disease. Fruit also helps your body to make the **energy** it needs to keep working all day and night.

Giant fruits

Of all the fruits that grow on trees, the jackfruit is the largest. This fruit has a greeny-yellow skin and banana-flavoured flesh. It can weigh up to 40 kilograms (over 80 pounds) and measure up to 1 metre (39 inches) long and 50 centimetres (20 inches) in diameter. Each jackfruit can also contain up to 500 seeds.

Why does fruit taste good?

Plants grow fruits that look, smell, and taste good to encourage animals to eat them and spread their seeds. When animals eat fruits with small seeds, they also swallow the seeds. The seeds later come out in the animal's **droppings**. If the seed is large, the fruit may be carried away and the seed dropped elsewhere. When the seeds grow somewhere new, the young plants that emerge won't compete with the parent plant for space and light.

Fruit ripens when the seeds inside are fully developed. This ensures animals do not eat the fruit before the seeds are ready to grow into a new plant.

When is a fruit not a fruit?

In scientific terms, some of the foods we call vegetables are actually fruits because they contain the plant's seeds. These include tomatoes, peppers, aubergines, and cucumbers. We call them vegetables because they do not taste sweet and we mainly eat them as part of a main meal. On the other hand, a few of the fruits we eat are not really fruits. For example, rhubarb is the stem and not the seed-bearing part of the rhubarb plant. We call it a fruit because we eat it sweetened as dessert.

How do fruits grow without seeds?

Some of the fruits you eat, such as some kinds of grapes, do not have seeds inside. Fruit growers grow them this way because some people prefer to eat seedless varieties. Seedless grapes are grown from cuttings of an unusual grape plant that grew fruit without any seeds. To grow more grape plants the same as this one, the fruit grower cuts a piece of stem from the plant and grows it into a new grape plant.

When farmers grow new plants from cuttings, the new plant will be identical to the first plant. So, if the first plant grew seedless grapes, the other plants will, too.

WHERE DOES FRUIT COME FROM?

Fruits grow on many kinds of plants. Some, including apples, figs, cherries, and oranges, grow on trees. Others, such as blackcurrants, blueberries, and gooseberries, grow on bushy plants. Grape and passion fruit plants have long, thin stems that wind themselves around other plants or supports to grow tall. Strawberry plants grow close to the ground.

 Many people think bananas grow on trees, but in fact banana plants have long leaves that grow from an underground stem.

Fruits around the world

Thousands of years ago, people ate fruit they found growing on wild plants. Later, people began to grow their favourite fruit plants. Almost all plants need soil, water, and light to grow, but some types of fruit grow better in different **climates**. People group these different types of fruits into **deciduous**, **citrus**, and **tropical** fruits. Today most people eat a wide variety of fruit all year round because it is **exported** in large container ships to all parts of the world.

Deciduous fruits

Deciduous fruits have a seed or seeds enclosed in a heavy stone surrounded by a soft flesh and **edible** skin. Deciduous fruit plants grow best in countries that have mild summers and cold winters, such as the UK and colder regions of North America. Deciduous fruit trees such as apples, pears, peaches, and cherries drop their leaves in autumn and rest throughout winter, which is why they can survive frosts.

Farmers grow many deciduous fruit plants in large orchards or fruit farms. The delicate fruits are usually harvested by hand.

Hard-working apple trees

Trees put in a lot of work to grow apples. It takes the **energy** produced by about 50 leaves to produce just one apple. Leaves create energy from water, sunlight, and carbon dioxide (a gas from the air). The tree uses this energy to grow and to produce fruit.

Citrus fruits

Citrus fruits have a thick, **inedible** peel. We eat the juicy flesh inside which grows in segments or sections. Citrus fruits include lemons, oranges, grapefruit, tangerines, and limes. The juice in citrus fruits contains **citric acid**. Lemons contain about four times as much citric acid as oranges, which is why lemons taste especially sharp or tangy.

Citrus fruits grow in warm places such as California, Spain, Morocco, and Israel. Citrus fruits stay fresh and juicy for a long time because of their padded protective skins, which is why many are exported.

Citrus fruit trees have dark green, waxy leaves and sweet-smelling flowers. Unlike deciduous fruit plants, they keep their leaves all year round.

Tropical fruits

Tropical fruits mainly grow in the very warm and wet climates of the Tropics, or in greenhouses that provide a similar climate. The Tropics is an area around the **Equator** with high temperatures all year round, and includes places such as South-east Asia, Africa, and South and Central America. Tropical fruits include mangoes, papayas, pineapples, and bananas. Many tropical fruits are soft and thin-skinned, so they bruise or squash easily. They have to be packed and transported to other parts of the world with great care.

Pineapples became popular in Europe after 1493, when Spanish explorers brought them home from the island of Guadeloupe. Pineapples look a bit like pine cones, so the explorers called them "pina". The English added "apple" to the name to show they were a fruit.

Banned fruit

The durian is a large tropical fruit with a hard spiky skin that contains soft edible flesh. Durian fans say the smell of the ripe flesh is fragrant, but many people find its strong odour offensive. In parts of South-east Asia, the fruit is banned from certain public places, such as hotels, restaurants, trains, and airlines, because of its smell!

WHY IS FRUIT GOOD FOR YOU?

Fruits are an important part of a healthy diet because they give you vital **vitamins**, **minerals**, and other **nutrients**. Fruit is also good to eat because it tastes delicious and there is so much variety to choose from.

Why are vitamins vital?

Vitamins are substances that your body needs and that you get from the food you eat. There are two main groups of vitamins: fat **soluble** and water soluble. Fat-soluble vitamins, such as vitamin A, are transported around the body in fat. Any vitamins that are not used immediately are stored in the **liver** and in body fat. Some vitamins, including vitamin C, travel around the body in water. Water-soluble vitamins that are not used pass out of the body in **urine**. That is why you need a daily supply of vitamin C from fruit.

Some vitamins in fruit help to keep your eyes, nose, throat, lungs, and skin healthy.

Vitamin	What is it good for?	What fruits is it found in?
Vitamin A	Good for eyesight, healthy skin, and bone growth, and helps to protect against infections	Peaches, apricots, passion fruit, nectarines, mangoes, and melons
Folic acid, a kind of B vitamin	Helps the body form red blood **cells**, which carry **oxygen** around the body	**Citrus** fruits such as oranges, grapefruit, limes, and lemons
Vitamin C	Important for the growth and repair of all body **tissues**, including muscles. It helps keep gums, teeth and muscles healthy, helps the body to fight infections, and helps the body heal cuts and wounds.	Citrus fruits, berries, papayas, and kiwi fruit

Sailors and scurvy

In the 1700s, many sailors became sick with a disease called scurvy while on long sea voyages. A doctor called James Lind realized that the sailors got scurvy because something was missing from their diet. He gave different sailors different foods and only those who ate lemons and oranges got better. We now know that scurvy is caused by a lack of vitamin C.

Vitamin C from fruit can boost your **immune system** and help you fight off colds.

What are minerals?

Minerals are essential nutrients that your body needs in small amounts to work properly.

Iron helps make healthy red blood cells. Good sources of iron are dried fruits such as raisins, prunes, dates, and apricots.

Potassium may help to maintain healthy **blood pressure**. It is found in bananas, prunes, dried raisins and apricots, melons, and orange juice.

Magnesium helps maintain healthy muscles and nerves, keeps your heart beating steadily, keeps bones strong, and supports your immune system. Sources of magnesium include bananas, kiwis, raisins, and blackberries.

 Drinking water is not the only way to keep your body's fluid levels in balance. Try eating some juicy fruits, too.

Why do we need fruits for fibre?

Fibre is not a nutrient and the human body cannot **digest** it, so the fibre in the fruit we eat simply passes through the body. However, fibre helps us to feel full so that we don't snack on unhealthy foods between meals. Fibre also absorbs water and helps food move smoothly through the body. This is important because it is unhealthy to have food waste in your body for too long. Fibre reduces the amount of fat the body absorbs. This helps prevent heart disease. It also helps move potential cancer-causing substances through the body quickly, before they have a chance to get into your system.

Fresh fruits, especially if eaten with the skin on, are a great source of fibre.

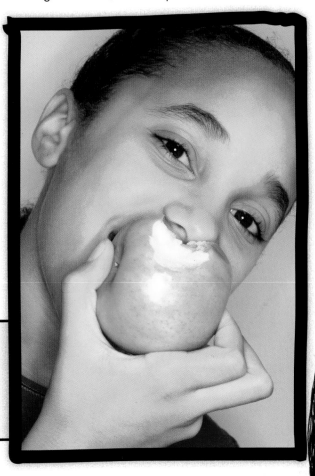

Juicy fruits

Most fruit contains about 80 percent water, but the juiciest fruits, such as melons, contain almost 90 percent water! Water is a vital nutrient for humans. There is water in the body's blood, saliva, and skin – in fact, there is water in almost every part of the body. You lose some water every day when you urinate and sweat, so it is vital that you replace it.

Why do athletes eat bananas?

Athletes eat bananas because they contain **carbohydrates**. Carbohydrates are nutrients that give people energy. Bananas are an especially good source of carbohydrate energy, but all fruits are useful sources of this body fuel.

Natural sugars, such as the fructose found in fruits, are forms of simple carbohydrates. When the body digests fruits, it breaks these foods down into glucose, which passes into the bloodstream. The blood carries glucose and oxygen (taken in when people breathe) all around the body. Inside the body's cells, the glucose and oxygen are mixed together to release energy.

Bananas are a good source of fructose, which can be broken down into glucose to fuel your body.

Apple-powered cars?

It seems that fruit may also be able to give vehicles energy to go. Some American scientists have said that in the future, fructose sugar found in fruits such as apples and oranges could be converted into a new type of fuel to power cars.

▲ Your body needs energy for absolutely everything you do, from sleeping to surfing. Fruit is one of the foods that can provide you with energy.

Does fruit contain fat?

Most fruit contains very little, if any, fat. That is why fruit can help you to maintain a healthy weight. Eating fruit is also a good way to enjoy the sweetness of sugar without the fat content of most other sweet foods. For example, there is half a gram (0.02 of an ounce) of fat in a banana, compared to at least 10 grams (0.35 of an ounce) of fat in a 40-gram (1.4-ounce) chocolate bar. Being over-weight can lead to health problems and an increased risk of disease, so this is another good reason to eat fruit instead of unhealthy alternatives.

WHAT IS THE BEST WAY TO EAT FRUIT?

 Try to eat fruit soon after you peel and chop it up. Fruit starts to lose some of its nutrients once it has been prepared.

All fruits are healthy to eat, whether fresh, juiced, cooked, canned, frozen, or dried. The important thing is to try different fruits to find out which you like, because then you are more likely to eat fruit on a regular basis.

Is fresh fruit best?

Fresh fruits have more **vitamins** and **minerals** than cooked or canned fruit. However, after fruit has been picked from the plant it starts to lose small amounts of some vitamins, so try to eat fruit soon after buying it. Frozen fruits are usually frozen soon after picking. They initially lose levels of some of their **nutrients** but then these levels remain constant while the fruit is frozen. Cooked or canned fruits contain useful nutrients, but you should avoid those that contain too many sugars or sweet syrups.

Fruit juice is a good source of vitamins, but juices are high in natural sugars and low in fibre. That is why juice should not be a complete alternative to fresh fruit. When fruits such as raisins and apricots are dried, the process reduces their vitamin C content. However, dried fruits still contain many other useful nutrients, making them a healthy choice as a snack. Just remember to read the label to check they do not contain added sugar.

The **bacteria** that spoil food need moisture to survive. When fruit is completely dried out, it lasts much longer than fresh fruit.

Square melons?

In Japan, people eat a lot of large, round watermelons, but these fruits are hard to pack for delivery, tricky to fit in a fridge, and roll around when you try to cut them. Now some farmers grow the melons in glass boxes so that the fruit naturally grows into a convenient cube shape.

Should you wash fruit?

It is a good idea to wash fruit before you eat it, to get rid of any bacteria or dirt that may have got onto the fruit since it was picked. Washing also gets rid of any traces of **pesticides**. These are chemicals some farmers spray on fruit to kill insect pests that might eat or damage the fruit. Rub the fruit with your fingers while holding it under running water. Washing is not important for fruit such as oranges and bananas, which you always peel before eating.

 If possible, it is better to eat washed rather than peeled fruit, because the most nutritious part of the fruit is just below the surface of the skin.

Fruits are a great source of nutrients, but sugars from fruit can cause tooth decay and dried fruits stick to your teeth. Don't forget to brush your teeth after eating fruits.

Is organic fruit better?

Organic fruit farms grow fruit plants without using artificial chemicals. Instead, they grow plants that attract certain insects. These insects eat the pests that might eat or damage the fruit. Some people think that organic food is safer to eat than food that is grown using pesticides, but both organic and conventional fruits are healthy and equally nutritious. It is a matter of personal choice which you eat.

Fruit snacks

Here are some new ideas for healthy fruit snacks.

To make healthy ice pops, freeze puréed soft fruit such as mango or papaya, or fruit juice, in ice cube trays or paper cups with wooden sticks.

Mix up a bag of your favourite dried fruits, such as apple slices, raisins, and cranberries.

Slice bananas into thin rounds and spread them on a baking tray. Cover with cling film and freeze to make banana bites! Try this with grapes or berries, too.

HOW MUCH FRUIT SHOULD YOU EAT?

Fruit is a vital part of a healthy diet and you should eat at least five portions of fruit and vegetables a day. Eat fruit with breakfast, as snacks, and in or after main meals, and try a variety of different kinds.

What is a portion of fruit?

One portion of fruit weighs about 80 grams (3 ounces) after you have removed all the bits you cannot eat such as the peel. That is equivalent to:

- one apple, banana, pear, orange, or similar sized fruit
- two plums or similar sized fruit
- one slice of a large fruit such as melon or pineapple
- three heaped tablespoons of fruit salad or stewed fruit
- one heaped tablespoon of dried fruit such as raisins
- one handful of grapes, cherries, or berries
- one 150-milliltre (5-fluid-ounce) glass of fruit juice. Limit fruit juice to a maximum of one portion a day.

Top tips

Here are some ideas for getting more fruit into your daily diet.

- Drink a glass of 100 percent fruit juice and add berries or sliced banana to your cereal for breakfast.
- Eat an apple or other fruit with your lunch.
- Snack on some grapes or raisins.
- After dinner, eat some pineapple or mango for dessert.

A balanced diet

Fruit is only one of the foods you need to eat. A balanced diet contains a variety of foods that together provide all the **nutrients** people need to be healthy. The Eatwell plate diagram below shows the types and proportions of foods needed for a well-balanced diet. It shows that people should eat:

- lots of fruit and vegetables
- plenty of grains and other **starchy carbohydrate** foods, such as bread, rice, pasta, and potatoes
- some milk and dairy foods
- some meat, fish, eggs, beans, and other non-dairy sources of **protein**
- just a small amount of foods and drinks that are high in fat or sugar.

The Eatwell food plate shows the proportion of food from each food group you should eat to achieve a healthy, balanced diet. This takes account of everything you eat, including snacks.

Fruit recipes

Blueberry muffins

Blueberries are a particularly nutritious fruit. These small indigo-blue fruits are a rich source of **fibre** and **vitamins** A and C.

Ingredients

- 250 g (9 oz) self-raising flour
- 1 teaspoon baking powder
- 50 g (2 oz) butter
- 75 g (3 oz) caster sugar
- 175g (6 oz) fresh blueberries
- Grated rind of 1 lemon
- 2 eggs
- 250 ml (8 fl oz) milk

Equipment

- 12 muffin paper cases
- 12-hole muffin tin
- Mixing bowl
- Wooden spoon
- Jug
- Fork
- Tablespoon
- Oven gloves
- Wire rack

WHAT YOU DO

1 **Preheat** the oven to 200 °C/ 400 °F/gas mark 6. Put the muffin paper cases into the muffin tin.

2 Put the flour and baking powder into the mixing bowl. Add the butter. Use your fingertips to rub the butter and dry ingredients together until the mixture looks like fine breadcrumbs.

Always ask an adult to help you in the kitchen.

3 Stir in the sugar, blueberries, and grated lemon rind.

4 Use a fork to mix the eggs and milk together in a jug. Pour this mixture into the mixing bowl and stir with a wooden spoon until well mixed. (It will still look a bit lumpy.)

5 Use the tablespoon to spoon the mixture into the paper cases. Fill each paper case almost to the top.

6 Bake the muffins in the oven for about 20–25 minutes until they have risen and turned golden. Leave the muffins to cool for a few minutes in the tray. Carefully lift them out and place them on a wire rack to cool them for a little longer before serving.

Fruit smoothie with a fruit kebab

Make a banana and mango smoothie and decorate it
with a fruit kebab!

Ingredients

For the kebabs:
- 1 apple
- 4 tablespoons red seedless grapes
- 4 tablespoons green seedless grapes
- 8 tablespoons pineapple chunks

For the smoothies:
- 1 mango
- Half a banana
- 125 ml (4 fl oz) vanilla yogurt
- 250 ml (8 fl oz) milk

Equipment

- Knife
- Chopping board
- 3 wooden skewers
- Large plate
- Blender
- Glasses

WHAT YOU DO

1 Prepare the fruit first. Remove the grapes from their stalks and wash them under cold water. Wash the apple and cut it into small squares, about 1 cm (one-third of an inch) across. If the pineapple is fresh, cut off its skin and take out the tough central core. Then cut it into chunks, too. Put the fruit onto a large plate.

2 Put pieces of fruit onto one of the skewers.

Always ask an adult to help when using tools such as sharp knives and blenders in a kitchen.

EAT SMART

You can put the fruit on in any order you like, but it looks attractive if you mix it up. Do this until the stick is almost covered from end to end.

3 Repeat these steps with two more skewers.

4 To make the smoothie, peel the mango, cut away its stone, and put the fruit into a blender. Peel the banana and put it in the blender together with the yogurt and milk. Whizz all the ingredients together until smooth.

5 Pour the smoothie into three glasses. Garnish each glass with a fresh fruit kebab and serve immediately.

Apple crumble

Cooking apples cannot be eaten raw, but they are nutritious and good to eat when cooked. You could try serving this crumble with yogurt or a little vanilla ice cream.

Ingredients

- 2 large cooking apples
- 50 g (2 oz) sultanas or raisins
- A large pinch of cinnamon or mixed spice
- 50 g (2 oz) brown or white sugar
- 100 g (4 oz) plain flour
- 50 g (2 oz) butter or margarine
- 75 g (3 oz) rolled oats

Equipment

- Weighing scales
- Sieve
- Peeler
- Sharp knife
- Chopping board
- Mixing bowl
- Measuring spoons
- Ovenproof pie dish

WHAT YOU DO

1 Preheat the oven to 190 °C/ 360 °F/gas mark 5.

2 Sieve the flour into a bowl.

3 Use your fingertips to rub the butter into the flour. Keep doing this until the mixture looks like fine breadcrumbs.

4 Stir in the oats and add 25 g (1 oz) of the sugar.

5 Peel the apples, remove the cores, and chop the fruit into large chunks.

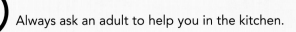

Always ask an adult to help you in the kitchen.

6 Place the apples, sultanas, and cinnamon in the pie dish and cover with the rest of the sugar (25 g or 1 oz).

7 Spread the crumble mixture over the apples.

8 Put the pie dish in the oven and bake for 40–45 minutes until golden brown.

GLOSSARY

bacteria extremely small organisms that can only be seen using a microscope. Some bacteria can cause disease or sickness.

blood pressure force exerted by the heart in pumping blood around the body

carbohydrate type of nutrient found in food. The body breaks carbohydrates down into sugars that it uses for energy.

cell all living things are made up of millions of microscopic parts called cells. Different parts of the body are made up of different types of cells.

citric acid substance found in citrus fruits. It is a natural preservative and gives citrus fruit its sharp, tangy flavour.

citrus family of fruits that include grapefruits, lemons, limes, and oranges

climate normal weather patterns of a region that occur year after year

deciduous plant that loses its leaves at the end of its growing season. Deciduous fruits have a seed or seeds enclosed in a heavy pit or stone surrounded by a soft flesh and edible skin.

diabetes people with diabetes are unable to turn sugars from their foods into energy, so they become very weak and tired

digest the name for the way the stomach, intestine, and other body parts work together to break down food into pieces so small they dissolve in liquid and pass into the blood

droppings animal faeces or waste matter

edible safe to eat

energy people require energy to be active and to carry out all body processes, including breathing. Plants require energy from the sun to make food by photosynthesis.

Equator imaginary line around the centre of the Earth. On maps, the Equator divides the Earth into a northern hemisphere and a southern hemisphere.

export transport and sell goods to a foreign country

fibre part of food that cannot be digested but helps to keep the bowels working regularly

immune system the human body's system of defences against disease. The immune system includes white blood cells and antibodies that react against bacteria and other harmful material.

inedible something that cannot be eaten because it would make you sick

liver body part located inside the body below the chest. The liver cleans the blood and produces bile, a substance that helps break down food in the digestive system.

mineral substance that comes from non-living sources, such as rocks that break down and become part of the soil. Some of the nutrients that plants take in through their roots are minerals.

nutrient substance found in food that is essential for life

organic describes food that is grown without the use of artificial fertilizer or pesticides

oxygen a gas in the air

pesticide chemical that farmers use to control animal pests, such as beetles, which damage their crops

preheat to heat an oven to the recommended temperature before cooking in it

protein nutrient that provides the raw materials the body needs to grow and repair itself

seed plant part that can grow into another plant. Most plants make flowers, which eventually turn into fruit. The seeds are inside the fruit. Seeds can be spread by wind, water, or animals.

soluble substance that can be dissolved in liquid

starchy something containing starch. Starch is a plant's store of excess glucose (food).

tissue group of similar cells that act together to perform a particular job. For example, skin cells form skin tissue.

tropical region close to the Equator that has a warm and damp climate. Tropical fruit grows in tropical regions.

urine liquid waste which you pass out of the body when you urinate

vitamin nutrient people require to grow and stay healthy

FIND OUT MORE

At **www.eatwell.gov.uk** there is a wide range of information including tips on eating healthy foods and keeping food safe.

The BBC website **www.bbc.co.uk/health/healthy_living/nutrition** covers many aspects of healthy eating.

At **www.childrenfirst.nhs.uk/teens/health/healthy_eating** there are sections on healthy eating and the digestive system, and a body mass index calculator to find out if you are a healthy weight.

At **kidshealth.org/kid** there is a large section on staying healthy and some recipes to try.

Click on the 'Healthy eating' link at **www.nutrition.org.uk** for ideas for healthier lunches, a closer look at the Eatwell plate, and more.

INDEX